Leadership

The Ultimate Guide To Being A Great Leader.

Achievement Pyramid

Table of Contents

Introduction 3
What Is Leadership? 5
The Importance Of Being A Leader 14
An Art In Itself 20
Empowering Your Team 24
Leading Effortlessly 29
Leading Teams 38
Building Your Network 45
Leadership Styles 49
Conclusion 57

Introduction

What does it take to be a good leader? Perhaps you've been recently promoted at work, or maybe you're the boss of a business. It could be you've been in a leadership position for a long time, whether in retail, the service industry, production, human resources, education, finance, a blue chip company, or maybe even as a line manager. The possibilities are endless.

Or maybe you're quite new to this leadership role you've been given. Either way, we can all do with some advice, whether it's just to brush up on our leadership skills, be reminded of important principles, or even to be pointed in the right direction as you start out on this path.

Leadership is not always easy, but it doesn't have to be extremely difficult either! In this book I will share with you a range of vitally important leadership principles; principles which apply across virtually every field. Whether you're the boss, a line manager or in charge of your own department you will find that applying this advice will make a big difference to you and your staff.

I want this chapter to be accessible to everyone, so there's nothing complex or too difficult to understand in here. Just tried and trusted, solid, sensible guidance that WILL help you be a better, more effective leader - whatever your job!

What Is Leadership?

Leadership is a broad concept and it is expressed in varying ways within several environments; the specific tasks may differ between a mom trying to ensure her son makes it to soccer practice and a moderately successful tech entrepreneur looking to launch her company on the stock market. However at the nucleus of their task would be these two concepts: a specific goal and mobilizing other people towards this goal. Leadership therefore can be simply defined as the ability to mobilize, coordinate, motivate, direct and manage people towards achieving a specific goal. And the core competence to getting this done is; Influence.

The Most Common Misconceptions About Leadership

Leadership is actually one of those concepts that can be easily misunderstood; for some; it is seen as lording over people; commanding their respect and forcing through the achievement of a specific goal. For others it is creating jovial connections with others and hoping to cajole them towards a particular goal. On whichever side of this pendulum your choice swings in defining leadership; if your goal is to be a true leader, you would find immense value in adopting a functional approach to thoroughly understanding the concept.

Despite it being one of the most important roles, shaping the face and personality of a company, not many people understand what leaders actually do. To better understand what leadership is, let's first take a look at what it's not.

Here are some of what people think about leaders; which are not entirely correct.

Misconception 1: Leaders have titles According to John C. Maxwell, Leadership Authority, "True leadership cannot be awarded, appointed or assigned. It comes only from influence, and that cannot be mandated. It must be earned. The only thing a title can buy is a little time – either to increase your level of influence with others or to undermine it."

Leadership is often associated with seniority and impressive titles. While being in a position of power can make leading easier, it is not enough. It's also not necessary - you don't have to be the Chief Executive of your company to lead. Leaders exist on all levels of society. A leader can be anyone with a great idea, a particular talent, who can think creatively or has a vision and a passion to make other people follow. Some are employees, teachers, parents or football coaches. Some are CEOs, Presidents or Sergeants. The ability to exercise social influence is what matters. Have you not seen those groups where the leader with the title, is not the one the group follows? If leadership were about positions then there would never be dissent, countries would not have coups and everyone would simply flow in the direction of the group head who would have somehow gathered influence because of a promotion or appointment to lead. If you are given a position; your job as in attaining leadership is not done, in fact, it may just be starting.

Misconception 2: All leaders are extroverts Some personality traits tend to be associated more with leadership than others. The extroverted personality is one of them: Openness, outspokenness and sociability are valued traits in today's society often associated with a strong will and ability to lead. However, nothing indicates that extroverts should make any better leaders than introverts. Abraham Lincoln, one of the most visionary and loved leaders, was for example a known introvert. Leadership doesn't only require good people's skills (something that can be learned) but also demands deep thought, willingness to listen carefully and a high level of focus; something that introverts tend even be better wired for. No matter what your personality type is, it has no proven direct correlation with your ability to lead.

Misconception 3: There can be only one leader Another common misconception about leadership is that there can be only one leader. Even though many companies adopt this approach, it is far from the only or most beneficial way to run things. As Tom Peter observed, "the best leaders don't create followers; they create more leaders." Supporting emerging leaders is a strategy that in the long run will result in better quality work as more leaders will unburden each other while giving a second opinion on difficult matters. Leading often involves moving through unknown territory with no definite answers or fool proof strategies. While a single, authoritarian ruler can only deal with one obstacle or short lived opportunity at the time, multiple leaders can share the workload and ensure that nothing is overlooked. As mentioned before, leaders don't need to be appointed. They might simply be great employees with a vision who can help inspire and direct fellow employees. Creating more leaders can help everyone learn together and support each other in ever faster changing surroundings. Top-down leadership is an outdated style that works with authority, not influence, and it will only get you so far. Sharing leadership makes us smarter and better capable of handling change in the long run.

Misconception 4: Leaders do better if they are rewarded more highly than others. Even though some leaders get a higher wage and have authority over others, this isn't what makes them leaders. Followers tend to dislike leaders who care too much about their luxurious hotel rooms and only go to work to decide over others. Good leaders aren't motivated by perks but by their passion for what they are doing.

Misconception 5: Leadership is the same thing as management Leadership and management are two terms that are often used interchangeably as if they are the same. Nothing could be more wrong. Leadership and management are two completely different things that need completely different skillsets. Management is about planning, delegating, coaching and making things happen. They ask themselves how they can make something work. What processes and tools do we need? Who needs to do what? While leaders need to do many of those things, too, their most important task is something else. They ask themselves why. Working from a philosophical perspective, they dream up visions, influence people around them and empower and inspire them to come along. They don't deal only with the practicality of models and systems in the same way that managers do.

Warren Bennis, a professor at the University of Southern California, brilliantly explained the main difference between managers and leaders: "Managers do things right but leaders to the right thing."

So, even though management could be a role played by the leader, the task of leadership transcends the technicalities of management to border on certain higher intangibles that decide influence and determine success.

The definition of Leadership

Even though Warren Bennis" definition describes the essence of leadership, it still does not capture the concept holistically. To define it with everything it entails, it"s important to look at all aspects of what a leader is supposed to do.

According to serial entrepreneur Kevin Kruse "leadership is a process of social influence, which maximizes the efforts of others, towards the achievement of a goal." He believes that all three aspects of this definition – social influence, others" effort and the achievement of a goal - are important parts of being a leader and that none of them should be left out. Let us explore this definition in more detail:

Exercising social influence Social influence is the ability to create a general acceptance of your view point within a group of two or more people. It is the uncanny ability to prevail in thought and therefore influence their willful actions. Social influence can be expressed in several ways; from focusing the attention of a team on a specific goal or simply just getting people to dress different. At its best; social influence is the ability to have people independently own the specific aspirations and perspectives of the influencer as their own. It is therefore the job of a leader to find the ways the predetermined goals are important to each individual within a group such that working towards the achievement of the vision is primarily seen as working for one's self. Social influence therefore transcends the positional authority of any single individual but has to do with the authority wielded in the hearts of others. For example; a military commander is not necessarily a leader if he can only make his followers obey from the authority his title gives him. Good leaders know how to influence their followers in other ways.

Maximizing effort It is one thing to convince people about a specific goal and make them want to do it; it is another thing to have them do their very best towards achieving it. In life people have moments; their highs and lows. Sometimes at the end of a very well-articulated speech; people tend to feel motivated to do certain things. This motivation often turns out to be false and when reality bites, so often, their commitment begins to waver. If they have already agreed to be a part of the leaders goal; they may be unwilling to affect their relationship by doing a U- turn on that decision; but then they decide to approach it with very low energy, they are uncreative and are all but inactive within the group. A leader has the responsibility of fixing this; leading shouldn't just be about getting involved in the process; a true leader is able to make his followers maximize their effort by ensuring the goal is actually relevant to them and remains so.

Moving towards a common goal Leading would be pointless without a goal. A leader is someone who leads his followers towards a goal they all believe will result in a better future for them. As such, a leader's responsibility would be to keep the goal in the consciousness of each individual within the group. This would entail painting a clear picture of the expected outcomes of the goal and how it would improve the reality of every member of the group.

Big Question; Are Leaders Born or Made? In this chapter we have looked at what defines a leader. We now know what he looks like and can tell him apart from other authorities and managers. He is a visionary, capable of influencing the people around him to move towards a common goal. The big question now is: Are leaders born or are they made? Can anyone exercise social influence, go in front and inspire followers or is it reserved for just a few natural talents? Erika Andersen, founding partner of Proteus International, have observed that even though some people are born leaders, most of them learn over time through practice.

The Importance Of Being A Leader

One of the most important questions I'm asked on a daily basis, is "What does the word leadership even mean?" To put it simply, leadership is the process of directing the people around you, by influencing the way people feel, the way they act, and the way they even think. The perfect leader is one that can help lead people in a certain direction that all will benefit from it and one who can inspire the people around them to become the best that they can be. Without leadership, our entire world would quickly disintegrate and fall into chaos. Why? Because every person on the planet views the world differently. As such they'll think, behave, and act differently than many people around them. A leader can help bring together these differences and have every person who follows them to work towards one common goal.

Leadership helps unite every person, regardless of ethnic background, skin color and religion. Becoming a great leader isn't something that happens overnight. Even those in history that we know are great leaders once had trouble securing a loyal following. An example of one such leader is Winston Churchill. When he arrived on the scene in the early 1930's, he tried to warn his people that Hitler was an imminent threat and one that should be taken seriously. As luck would have it, many people didn't see it that way. Many thought that Hitler was a man they could reason with, and many didn't want to start an unnecessary war with Germany. Of course they were all wrong, but still because of his proclamations many people shunned Winston Churchill for him trying to get those to believe that war would be inevitable as long as Hitler led Germany.

As luck would have it, many people rejected Churchill's claims and rejected him as a leader. Everything all changed the moment Germany overstepped their boundaries and began invading other countries. It was only then that people began following Churchill and sought his wisdom on what should be done. Eventually Churchill became Prime Minister of the United Kingdom and led the country into World War II. It was then that nearly every person residing in the United Kingdom followed him with willing faith and loyalty.

While Churchill is an example of a great leader, there are times in our own lives where we will need to be cautious of what I like to call false leaders. These kinds of leaders like to pretend that they are bringing people together toward a common goal when they really aren't. The truth of the matter isn't every person is destined to become a great leader. There are some of us who just don't have the necessary skills and attributes that makes a great leader. These people often try to lead the people around them, claiming they are able to inspire thousands while that is simply not the case. These people are often pretending they can do these things when in all reality they can't.

Leadership is something that can either cause greatness in many people or something that can cause great evil in many people. A prime example of this is Hitler himself, who, let's face it, was a great leader. He somehow managed to inspire people to participate in the deadliest mass genocide and not once did his own people speak against this act. Hitler was able to inspire these people to conduct such heinous acts and they all followed him without question.

Another example of a great leader that uses his power for the main purposes of hurting those around him is a leader in the business world. These kinds of leaders are known for abusing their power and using it to exploit the people around them. For example, in a non-profit organization many leaders have been known to use their power to benefit themselves rather than the people they are supposed to be helping.

It's important to know that abusing the power of leadership can cause harm to the people who you want to help because it will help you to become the best leader you can be regardless if you're at home or at work. You need to understand that leadership is power and in order to be used the right way, you need to make sure that you lead people in the right and positive direction.

What Is The Importance of Leadership?

There are a number of reasons as to why leadership is important regardless of where the skill is being utilized. Some of these reasons include:

1. **Provides Direction.** This can be extremely important especially for those who do not know or understand which direction they are supposed to be

working towards. This is incredibly important during times that are unstable in both our personal and professional lives and there will be times when people are going to look to you for some kind of guidance on what they should do.

2. Provide Stability and a Safe Environment. As adults at home and as supervisors in the workplace, we're often looked up to in order to provide some stability in the place and to provide a safe environment for both children and co-workers. You'll need to be responsible for teaching your children how to become well-rounded and self-sufficient adults and you'll be the person your co-workers will look to when they need to be reassured and motivated in the work place.

3. To Provide Guidance On How To Follow Their Passions. Neither children and adults are any exception to this rule. In order to become self-sufficient and happy adults, people need to follow their passion, to wake up every day feeling successful. You'll play a key role in making this dream a reality, and can even help in motivating those around you to follow their passions.

4. **Provide a Sense of Balance.** It's rather difficult to create the perfect balance between our personal and professional lives. As a leader, you can help the people around you to find that perfect balance (even if you don't have it yourself) and help them from becoming overwhelmed on a daily basis.

There's a greater need these days for people to recognize their true potential and to recognize whether or not they have the necessary skills to become a leader and to achieve greatness in their everyday lives. As I have stated multiple times, some people are not destined to become great leaders, but that does not mean they cannot rise above those around them and strive to become a leader in the future. Anything is possible with the right attitude and motivational drive in order to make the dream a reality. Ordinary people like you and me have the power to inspire change, to motivate the people around us, regardless of the circumstance and can help solve problems that other people usually cannot solve. We can lead others on a path that we want them to follow as long as we have the right mindset to do so and we can help these people work towards a better future in the long run.

An Art In Itself

Leadership principle number two may, on the face of it, seem to be slightly contradictory to what we've just looked at in principle one. However, I hope you'll see that's not at all the case. Whilst we must always treat our staff well, it is also very important that leaders are FIRM when they need to be.

There's sometimes a fear that if we're too nice to our staff they will seek to take advantage of this. Perhaps they will mistake your niceness for weakness, and attempt to take liberties. Now, in some instances, and with certain people, this may happen. However, the way in which you deal with it will determine whether or not it continues...

Remember that whilst it is important to treat your staff well, it's also vital that you're firm and unwavering when you have to be. You are the leader, which means you are responsible when things don't run smoothly, and it's up to you to find solutions. If a bad attitude amongst some of your staff is the problem, then you need to address it. Becoming firm but fair leaders, that others trust, is at the heart of sustaining effective leadership.

One of the things that you need to do is to be clear about your expectations and standards. As we've said, some of your staff may take liberties and push their luck in the workplace. They may shirk their responsibilities, fail to follow directives, produce shoddy work, be lax about timekeeping, and so on.

Let's be clear, as a leader you cannot afford to be weak. Don't let small problems build up into big problems through lack of action. Remember, there's a big difference between being fair, engaging with your employees, and being weak and fawning over them.

Deal swiftly and firmly with anyone who has a bad attitude. Don't let people mistake your 'niceness' for weakness. It's not. Call them in for a meeting and outline the problem, and what needs to be done to rectify it. Be firm and assertive when you need to be - without being rude or aggressive. It's the classic case of 'the iron fist in a velvet glove.'

Also, when you're outlining your expectations, be specific – your message will have greater impact if it is clear and direct. Always be upfront, direct and honest;

and maintain an attitude that is communicated in a mature and controlled way.

When you need to address a problem then stand or sit upright and tall, but in a relaxed manner; and don't be afraid to look people calmly in the eyes. Open hand gestures convey honesty and are disarming. When speaking, use a steady, calm tone in your voice that is not emotional. If the other person raises their voice, stay calm and don't raise yours. Remember, be firm, and continue to repeat your expectations if you have to.

I'd like to share a very helpful and insightful quote that I came across recently, and it sums up what we've covered in principles 1 and 2. It's this:

"To know when to be generous and when to be firm, that is wisdom." (Elbert Hubbard)

I hope you'll agree that is very good advice - particularly for someone in a position of leadership!

Let's briefly summarize what we've covered in this chapter before we move on any further. Remember the importance of being clear with your staff about your expectations. When those standards aren't met you need to make sure that you deal with any unacceptable behavior, but as you do this it's important to always stay calm and controlled. Ultimately, your goal is to ensure your staff recognize that you are a leader who is firm, but always fair.

So, although principle 1 stressed the need to treat your staff well; it's important to remember that there will also be times when, as a leader, you will have to BE FIRM. This is a key principle for the successful leader.

Empowering Your Team

In the words of that great philosopher – Elsa, "Let it go!"

What does it mean to empower someone? And while I realize there are several ways to answer this question, let's start with a good old fashion definition straight from the dictionary.

Here's how the Merriam Webster dictionary defines empower:

- To invest with power. Especially legal power or official authority.
- To equip or supply with ability; enable.

Sounds easy enough - right? I mean, what's hard about equipping people with what they need to do their job? Well, when you really break it down, it's not quite that simple. To truly empower someone means letting go, allowing others to make decisions and many times make mistakes. It means trusting that someone, other than yourself, can actually achieve success. After all, this is why you hire and pay staff.

I actually heard a beautiful example of empowerment from a good friend of mine named Amie. Amie was given the opportunity to take a leadership role within a new organization. She was so excited about what this company was capable of that she literally couldn't wait to walk through the door for the first time. Imagine her surprise when she found that practically every person on her team hated their job and did little more than punch the clock to get a paycheck.

She couldn't understand it! This company had so much potential! Why couldn't they just see it? So Amie did some digging. It didn't take long for her to figure out that her team was discouraged by the lack of internal promotions, training opportunities and company awards. Add to that, it was rumored that management didn't trust employees to carry out the mission of the organization. From the staff perspective they felt like they had never been given the chance to even try! This did not make for a happy or engaged bunch.

What did Amie do? She laid out a plan. Her first step was to enlist the assistance of a long-term employee to help her delve deeper into the reality of the situation they faced. She mentioned that the company had a history of failing to use their employees to their full potential. Upper management never asked for ideas or opinions and they weren't known for sharing any aspect of the decision making process. Even in the earliest stages. This left their team members feeling like drones. Like they had no purpose other than checking boxes and completing busy work, a reality that proved very frustrating, especially to the more senior staff.

So Amie decided to try a different approach. She made a point to communicate with every employee that they would have an equal opportunity when it came to promotions and other opportunities. She just had one requirement. If you wanted to be selected for advancement then you had to aid in the success of the organization. She expected every single one of her team to step up and lead when necessary.

If there was a decision to be made then she demanded not only accurate analysis but also well thought out recommendations for potential courses of action. This was required and everyone had to participate. They had to become part of the process!

Her thought was simple. "I'll provide you with the resources, remove any barriers and empower you with authority. You deliver the product that blows management away."

Her next step centered around follow-up. Amie took time every single day to talk with her employees, both giving them feedback and providing encouragement. She felt these were crucial factors to empowering and enabling them to do their very best. The result? Her team was able to achieve things they never thought possible. They were astoundingly successful. Far beyond the corporate expectation.

The lesson here? If a person, or team, is adequately empowered they have the potential to move mountains. Things they initially feel are impossible become well within their grasp. The key is they must be given the resources and authority to actually do these things. They have to be empowered.

Leadership in Action:

How do you put this into play in your daily role? Here are a few key tips.

- Treat your team members like adults.
- They are not your children and they have no desire to be micromanaged on a daily basis. Yes, this

means giving up a measure of control but the long-term rewards for this action are immeasurable.

➤ Set realistic expectations for both yourself and your team.

➤ Set goals that will stretch your expectations and capabilities, but not break them. Find that fine line and learn how to walk it.

➤ Coach effectively my resolving issues without removing responsibility.

Part of empowering others means being self-aware and to taking ownership of mistakes and outcomes. Failure is often a stepping-stone to success. It is how you handle that failure that will determine if the success is ever realized. Be forgiving of mistakes and use them as opportunities to both teach and learn.

Leading Effortlessly

If you are easy to follow, many of the difficult elements of leadership become easier—or even effortless. Through your values, you can build a culture where some common team problems don't (or can't) develop. And the team can behave in a manner they know will please you, even when you are not there.

Identifying your values shows everyone what's truly important. When you invite your team's buy-in concerning these values, and if you work with them to choose the team's values, you and your team will understand each other better and see each other's authenticity more clearly.

Why Do People Follow Values Over Skills?

People follow values over skills because they relate to them, agree with them, and recognize that they give meaning to life and to their efforts at work—they are ultimately the reasons why we are all here. Connecting with someone's values can be an emotional, impactful experience. Skills don't connect people or impact people at an emotional level, typically. They just aren't important enough.

There is magic in declaring the values that are important to you—verbally, through your actions, or in writing. The moment you express that something like honesty is important, honesty becomes a more active part of your daily practice. Others hold you accountable just by seeing you and don't have to say anything. It's the accountability of no accountability. It's automatic. Clear values guide us in the way our habits do; we barely have to think about them.

Values become not only visible but central to the work when they are recognized; no one needs a class or conference to achieve that. It doesn't even need to show up on your company's budget. This is the only leadership development that truly works—and it's free.

This level of leading is effortless. It transparently aligns actions and intentions and enables others to align with you. It allows you to have the impact you seek on those who depend on you, workplace teams and loved ones alike. Leading effortlessly with values has no particular form. You don't even create it. It's already there. The effort may come in identifying the values, living the values, and recognizing them in others—all of which require a level of being present, or mindfulness. You need to have that list of values in your mind when an opportunity presents itself.

Why Does Learning Skills and a Conventional Leadership Development Approach Make You Harder to Follow?

How have you experienced leadership development where you work?

Leaders are quite commonly given a skill to learn. This comes in many forms. Sometimes it's their boss forwarding a link to an article. Other times, leaders are given direction as part of an annual goal to attend a conference or class. Other forms this can take are more ad hoc; an organization schedules a class or retreat and brings in something timely and/or short term.

Leaders will usually learn whatever this is and try it on with their teams with little context. It's like showing up one day, and suddenly sporting a moustache or a hat. People who are close to you may ask you about it immediately. Others will wait patiently until you leave the room to ask others if they noticed the change, and everyone discusses what they think of it. Group dynamics won't usually play favorably when it comes to this. Generally, people are far more likely to commiserate and banter over things they don't like than talk about changes they love.

As an example, let's say a leader reads a book on conflict resolution. There are many great resources about how to resolve conflict or have difficult conversations; they mostly help with what to say to an adversary and why to say it. Most of the existing work in this area is based on very sound psychology. It's good. The problem is when the leader brings it to the environment that made the conversations difficult to begin with. This new sense of purpose and smooth phrasing to navigate the conversation is no more useful than that new moustache. To some, even if your intentions are totally pure, you will seem less authentic. This includes when you improve your own lousy habits and behavior—and it can get tricky.

I once worked with a manager who had such low scores on a multi-rater assessment (a 360 review, where people can anonymously rate their boss) in the area of trust, she wanted to quit. Conventional wisdom would be to get her to change her ways immediately with some actions that are associated with trust. The problem is that her sudden changes in behavior would be perceived as inauthentic. People didn't see her as sincere to begin with. This quickly becomes a catch-22: she can't stay in her current state, yet honest efforts to improve would further erode her standing.

This may be an unusual example, but it expresses the cautionary tale: skill development alone does not make you a better leader; it can do more damage than you think.

Learning Skills? Old Habits Die Hard

Why is change so difficult? There is no accurate data on how much money is spent on change management training and consultants, but it's a lot. William Bridges has a body of work in this area that has stood the test of time. One of his basic ideas is that it's not change people resist, it's the transition. He describes the difference between the two as change is an event, and transition is how we psychologically adapt to the event. While lots of planning and strategy focus on the change itself, the people who must carry it out are largely disregarded and yet they are the most important part of the initiative. They hold the key to its success or failure.

What this means on a deeper level is that we have our habits and how we behave is one of them. We all behave within a certain set of boundaries. If a change that must occur is clear and our role exists within these boundaries, it's easier for us to adapt. However, if we see this change as interfering with our values (i.e., the things we think of as important), we will resist change overtly, covertly, or sometimes even unconsciously.

When some leaders want to drive change, authoritarianism sometimes kicks in, and common explanations include "the bus is leaving the station with or without you, so be on it." Few things make it harder for a leader to be followed than forcibly telling others what is in their best interest. When leaders can connect a change to what's important to the person or the team (rather than convincing them why it's important and hoping they get it), it goes further.

Learning Skills? Attachment to Results

A very common part of being a leader is accountability to results. Inherent in this approach is to "drive results." This may even show up on some lists of corporate values. Driving results isn't really a value.

Your values, however, can naturally drive results if they are aligned.

Driving results implies there is resistance. When you are driving results, there is some level of extra effort described (it's not called "getting results" for a reason), and also implicit is that if you're not putting in this effort, results won't happen; ergo, results must be driven, pushed, or whatever.

Imagine a strong rope tied to the wall of a building. Pulling the rope actually gets an equal amount of resistance in the opposite reaction. Yet you may be pulling on such a rope thinking "Imagine if I wasn't pulling so hard, it would be flying in the other direction!" No it wouldn't.

If you don't pull the rope attached to the wall, it's still there, and it's still the same length. Driving results can sometimes mean a leader is leading too far out in front of the organization.

Attachment to results detaches you from the people. Driving results takes you away from growing or supporting the people, who in turn drive the results. Are you stepping on your people to drive results as "musts" and "mandatories"?

Learning Skills? I Learned Conflict Resolution, but No One Else Speaks This Language

When someone learns to speak the language of conflict resolution, it's a strong skill. Taking that skill back to an environment where existing boundaries, values, and use of language have made conflict the norm is largely ineffective. It's why months after this skill was learned (or the training was completed), there may be no difference in the nature of conflict in the environment. It's a waste.

If a leader focuses on the causes of unproductive conflict, it's more complicated, but a far better option—call it root-cause analysis. When a leader can learn why conflict is a problem on the team, that becomes a much easier endeavor. Rather than trying to get a person to act differently than their natural reaction to things, rather than giving people tools and hoping they all use them consistently and fairly, the leader with a Zen attitude knows that conflict is healthy. Instead of resisting it, support it.

Tools for managing conflict are usually geared toward ending or diffusing it. How about making conflict okay? Some great work has been written previously around supporting "well-managed conflict" in the workplace. When conflict is encouraged, people work through it much differently than making it akin to an argument where one person inevitably ends the interaction with "Let's agree to disagree." That solves nothing and does even less for positive relationships.

Leading Teams

When teams form in an organization, it is not to exchange or share information. With the advent of technology and communications, Information can be shared in a number of different way outside the setting of a group meeting. When teams meet, it is during a decision point in the process workflow. Efficient organizations and leaders know how to value the strengths of individuals and utilize the team setting for tasks that are better handled as a group rather than to disseminate individual assignments. Let's explore this topic some more.

Deciding on the structure of Teams: The makeup of the team varies, and so should your leadership style. This is a very broad topic because of the diversity of teams and leadership styles to deal with these teams as well as the diversity of projects and cultures across organizations. However, we should at least learn some basics. The most common types of team formations are:

1. Problem-Solving Teams: This is the typical small group structure across departments meeting with senior leadership or employees within the same department meeting with middle management. These teams meet regularly and discuss active problems, offer solutions, and give updates on past problems that are being actively resolved. There is a cadence to these meetings so as to structure a specific time to bring up problems to leadership.

2. **Independent Teams:** These are teams that don't need to report to senior leadership, and tackle problems directly as they arise. They are given authority and autonomy to solve problems as they see fit. The members of those teams are carefully chosen because they are motivated, driven, and have bought into the culture of the organization. You can spot them easily because they always refer to the company as 'our company' and the customers as 'our customers'.

3. **Cross-Functional Teams:** These are teams made up of experts from different business units in the department or company. They are usually brought together to work on a new project that requires everyone's input and buy-in. These teams can be difficult to manage because they are made up of educated, driven, ambitious individuals who consider themselves leaders in their respective fields.

Leading Type-A Highly Educated Individuals: This comes as no surprise that leading other 'leaders' is a challenge. Type A personalities are driven by complexity, challenge, and professional stimulation. They do not like to be led, and owing to the greater degree of expertise, the disadvantage is that they often reach conflict when trying to work together. The advantage of leading such an independent team is that the leader does not have to be the domain expert. In fact, the team prides itself in its own expertise. A cornerstone to one's interaction with such a team is making it clear that there is interdependence. This means that the clever team member's expertise will complement or supplement another member's expertise or even the leader's expertise. Establishing this interdependence early on has enabled better collaboration in a Harvard Business Review study of organizational leadership. After establishing that the team is interdependent, the leader's focus should shift from managing the discussion to one facilitating discussion. One approach is to use the nominal group theory of decision making with modifications when assigning tasks. This means asking for the input of the 'experts', taking their point of view into consideration, and asking them how soon they can deliver. As a leader of such a team, you will notice that they will relish the idea of finishing the deliverable before the deadline and will be even more excited if it was their solution that was chosen. Another important principle in this context is to demonstrate what's known as 'executive presence'. This means taking a step back from managing the details and projecting confidence that the team can handle the deliverable. Establishing interdependence, taking the role of facilitator, asking for their expert input, and demonstrating executive presence while remaining hands off will allow you to form a highly productive and efficient team.

4.   **Remote Teams:** In some organizations, the company talent is geographically separated. In such cases, the act of collaboration can be frustrating if the wrong technology is used. The members of such a team also lack competitive motivation because of minimal face to face interaction and do not initiate as much collaboration online as they would have if they were closer to each other. This is not to say that remote teams cannot work. They can. The challenges of this new work environment prompted a new research

discipline called computer supported cooperative work or network.

5. **Organizational Leadership:** This was how teams were formed a few decades ago. They were based on formal hierarchies and involved receiving routine predictable tasks from the boss. Idea generation, discussion, and decision making was reserved for the senior leadership only. While this works for routine tasks, it is less productive for new projects or tasks that require creativity or a change in operations. Additionally productivity has been show to correlate with buy-in from employees or what the literature refers to as Theory Y.

To paraphrase. Theory X is where expectations are set and performance is measured against those expectations, and Theory Y, is where a leader's job moved from setting expectations to providing all the necessary resources for their employees to do their best work. Theory Y is linked with the millennial generation that requires things like autonomy and a nurturing environment with a flat hierarchy to produce results. This goes back to our earlier emphasis on relationship building and emotional intelligence where leaders understand what motivates their employees and find that which inspires them to perform better.. Empirical research into the relationship between emotional intelligence and executive leadership was limited up until recently when researchers found that leaders with higher emotional intelligence were more likely to lead using transformative rather than transactional leadership.

6.   Matrix Structure: Initially seen in consulting firms, it is now a very common team structure. Employees in the matrix have more than one boss. They have the department manager who tasks them with the day to day duties and a project or program manager who was tasked with assembling his or her own team to complete a new project. This structure was created more so to separate the functional manager from the team leader so as to maximize their effectiveness with the employees. When recruiters advertise that they need someone comfortable with a matrix organization, they are explicitly asking for applications from individuals who feel comfortable wearing many different hats and reporting to different 'bosses'. This is a higher stress team organization, but for industries like consulting, it is important for efficiency to pull people from one project to another as needed.

Building Your Network

A leader's social network is an integral part of success. Organizational leaders are distinct compared to their counterpart managers in their ability to use their network to get things done. Networks are developed to improve operations, to accommodate the leader's career trajectory, or to support the business goals. What you'll find in the literature is by far, developing leaders fret over building social networks but those who overcome it are better for it. This inflection point of overcoming whatever personal reservations one has in building a robust network is pivotal in one's career. I want to stress that you should think of your social capital in the following three types of networking: operational, personal, and strategic. Let's look at how they differ.

Operational Networking: This comes most naturally by virtue of the work environment. Leaders have to work with their peers, their superiors, and a whole set of organizational characters. The operational network will help you produce results and then push you to the next stage of your career. The problem is that the old network is of no use to you in your new position.

Now what? That's why it is important to keep an open mind and build relationships with people who may not necessarily work with you today, but may work with you in the future, or whom you can leverage to build stronger relationships with different divisions. Build relationships across the aisle, don't stay in your own division.

Personal Networking: This one is the hardest for aspiring leaders. Many ask why spend additional time out of work to build relationships. The answer is simple: because people are what make or break your career. There are many get together from alumni events, company sponsored events, charities, volunteer groups, etc. Even if you do begin to spend part of your week building personal relationships, the question that comes up is whether you should talk to as many people as possible? Maybe you should see who is attending an event, then research their backgrounds so you have some talking points? No. This is not an operative mission and you are not undercover. The strongest relationships are those borne of similar interest. Additionally, conversation flows when you talk about something that interests you. You are not trying to using broad brush strokes. This network is meant to be stronger than your operational network. So much so, that if you're in a jam, or need mentoring, or need a referral or introduction, this is the network you would go to first.

Strategic Networking: This last network can take up the most time but also yield the most benefit. Strategic networking means actively picking the people whose support you want or who are key to moving you further in your career. Because this is not based on working together like operational networking, or based on mutual interests like personal networking, the strategic network requires much more leg work, one on one conversations, and even lending support to one of their causes so that they could lend support to yours down the line. As a leader moves up the ladder, they will find that they spend less time with operational networking and more time with strategic networking to build stakeholder support. Leaders at the very top spend a significant amount of time on speeches, meetings, discussions, etc.. to build support for themselves, for their ideas, and for their goals. Hopefully that answers the age old questions of when do senior leaders actually work? Strategic networking is their work. Start by thinking what your goals are, where you want to be, and whose support you want, then begin forcing these relationships slowly over months (and years sometimes) so as not to actually seem forced.

Leadership Styles

If you already know a bit about leadership, you may have heard about leadership styles. Traditionally, they have been used as a sort of personality test, making it easier for leaders to analyses what kind of leader they are, creating a better understanding of themselves and what they can accomplish with their own personal style. We are going to use a different approach and instead look at the different leadership styles within the context of The Situational Leadership Theory.

The Situational Leadership Theory According to the situational leadership theory developed by Paul Hersey, there is no single best leadership style. Instead there are a variety of different styles or strategies that all can be useful in different situations. A good leader will adapt his style to the needs of his team and project. As each team and project is different, a good leader will be able to analyses his company to combine the styles in a way that makes sense for them. The situational leadership theory offers a solution of how to properly decide which leadership style to use in which situation. The model is based on the relationship between leaders and followers and so can prove beneficial for everyone who is seeking to influence others. The strategy of the individual leader depends on various factors such as the amount of direction as well as emotional support given, the nature of the tasks involved, the organizational environment and the team members" skills, experience and level of motivation to perform a specific task. The situational leader will adapt his behavior based on these factors. With practice, you can learn how to switch instinctively. However, in the beginning it makes sense to analyses each case consciously to pick the right style. Here are four steps to remember when picking a leadership style for a specific situation:

1. Diagnose the situation and understand the circumstances of the people you are trying to influence.

2. Adapt your behavior to those circumstances.

3. Interact with others in order for them to understand and accept the changes.

4. Advance by managing the influence you are trying to exercise.

Whilst the situational leadership theory is widely used and agreed on, the different leadership styles vary. In this book we will introduce you to six of the most common leadership styles and explain when and how to use them. Maybe you already use some or more of these subconsciously but if you know about them, you can switch between them strategically according to the situation.

Goleman's six leadership styles A Harvard study led by Daniel Goleman and his team looked at 3000 middle-level managers and found six major leadership directions:

1. The pacesetting leader The pacesetting leader leads his team by being a good example himself. This works well for a self-directed team already motivated and autonomous. Team members are kept to a high standard as they are expected to follow the example of the leader. Those who need feedback and direction to perform don"t do well with pacesetting leaders and are often replaced if they can"t keep up. Used too much, this style can overwhelm team members and result in poor performance. There is usually no patience for learning or adjusting. The style should be used sparingly and only if you need good results in a short time from an already motivated team. If you keep using this style long-term, it will most likely result in stressed and dispirited team members. The Laissez-Faire style is another often mentioned leadership style that is similar in many ways to the pacesetting leader. It involves a lack of feedback and a great level of autonomy. Even though the leader here doesn't set himself as an example, the Laissez-Faire style often experience the same problems, resulting in poor production and increasing costs.

2. The authoritative leader The authoritative leader defines a common vision and can be used to unite an aimless team. It is then up to each team member to find his own method to get there. This style works well when the team is going in a new direction and have a need for a new vision instead of guidance. It inspires team members to come up with new ideas and sparks enthusiasm for the common goal. In Hay and McBers comprehensive study of thousands of executive, it proved to be the leadership style that created the happiest and most positive work environment The authoritative leadership style isn"t necessarily the best choice all the time, however. It can for example be difficult for a leader to emerge in a group of experts and make them follow his vision if they —maybe rightly — feel that they know better than him. The authoritative leadership style does well in the right situation but the leader has to use it with care and only when it makes sense.

3. The affiliate leader The affiliate leader takes care of his or her team members on an emotional level by praising them and creating a sense of belonging. This style can't be used on its own as too much nurture will result in a lack of motivation to work. However, it can be useful in stressful situations when the team feels overworked or have experienced a trauma. It is also more valuable than most people tend to think. Studies conducted by Hay and McBer showed that the affiliate leader actually has the second most positive impact on the work environment next after the authoritative leader. Even with the risk of underachievement, a caring leader results in a happy team. However, it works best together with a more result- oriented leadership style. Positive feedback, while encouraging, may result in underachievement and make team members continue down a wrong path if the leader isn't ready to correct mistakes or provide critical feedback.

4. The coaching leader The coaching leader trains his team and builds their skills to help them be more successful in the future. He will help them achieve their individual goals as well as create a plan to achieve them. He will assign tasks in agreement with the team members and won't mind giving them challenging assignments even if it means that it will slow down performance. Learning is valued more than performance in this case. The coaching leader will listen to the team's opinion but will make the final decisions himself. He will encourage and inspire them by creating a positive work environment, guide them and set clear expectations. This style needs a skilled leader, who genuinely cares about his team members improving in a direction that is useful for them, too. The leader has to have proficiency and his team members must be responsible and must be willing to learn and change. Even though it's considered a slow and tedious leadership style, its positive work environment actually often improve performance in the end. Team members feel more responsible, have less fear of experimenting, and are motivated to do their best. They often rise to the challenges given to them if they feel that their leader believes in them. As Daniel Goleman himself said: "Although the coaching style may not scream „bottom-line results", it delivers them."

5. The coercive leader This style is also called the autocratic leadership style. It's all about control and even though it was the most commonly used only a few decades ago, it has its limitations. A good leader is supposed to challenge the status quo, not just impose his or her own mind without regard for anything else. This style usually comes with a lack of trust in team members as they are not allowed to be a part of the process, express their opinions or have influence over their own jobs and it should only be used with care on rare occasions. It just won't work in most situations. Only use it if it's absolutely necessary, for example if you have to direct a team member who doesn't respond to any other leadership style or if he is very new and needs to focus on learning a new skill. It could also be used during an actual crisis such as a company turnaround or a fire. However, in most cases, this leadership style doesn't inspire unity or inventiveness but instead creates a rigid work environment that alienates the team members.

6. The democratic leader The democratic leader takes the ideas and opinions of his team members into consideration to facilitate a free flow of ideas. The leader lets the team take ownership of the project and involves them in the decision-making process while he sets the frame and guides them. This style is also called the participative leadership style because the members take a more participatory role in the company, but it only works if they are qualified to do so and if they are not working under time pressure. While the democratic leadership style is great to gain the most from a changing environment and explore all the ideas to go in the best possible direction, it's a slow process. When changes need to happen quickly, the democratic leadership style is not the way to go. However, if the company has got the time to make positive and lasting changes, the democratic leadership style has proven to create good results. It also has a positive impact on morale because the team members feel appreciated and valued for their opinions. It gives them the feeling that they are part of the process and can influence the future of the company.

Conclusion

In order to become a great leader in the long run, there are a variety of different things that you must do in order to have people follow of you. We discussed how honesty can play a critical role in how people view and respect you. You need to lead with kindness and love to increase that respect and you need to motivate the people around you so that all of you can work towards that common goal.

Motivation is just as important as leading the people that look to you for guidance. Without motivation our lives would be pretty dull. Without this, do not expect to become a great leader in the long run. Motivation is something that is needed on a daily basis especially if you wish to have a life that is running as smoothly as possible.

Keep in mind, not every person on the planet is destined to be a leader. Some of us do not have the necessary skills that is needed to be a leader. You need to understand that in order to become a great leader, a bit of science and steps need to be followed to allow for greatness. In order to become a great leader you need to use all of the tools and methods I have outlined correctly so that you can impact the people who follow you in the right way with motivation.

Hopefully by reading this eBook, you've learned everything there's to know about becoming a great leader, what are the necessary steps you need to take in order to reach the status of a great leader and how motivation itself can help you to become a great leader in the long run.

www.ingramcontent.com/pod-product-compliance
Lightning Source LLC
Chambersburg PA
CBHW071434220526
45469CB00004B/1531